It's Me, Achilles B

It's Time To Say Hello

MICHELLE A. BRAVO

Outskirts Press, Inc.
http://www.outskirtspress.com

ISBN: 978-1-4787-5525-8

Outskirts Press and the "OP" logo are trademarks belonging to Outskirts Press, Inc.

PRINTED IN THE UNITED STATES OF AMERICA

This Book Belongs to:

_____

To my children Christopher and Giavanna, my shining stars, you make my spirit whole. I love you both with all of my being.

To Nicholas, thank you for your love and devotion, how lucky are we to have each other and to Alice, who forever believes in my ability to soar.

To the inspiration for this book series, my Giant Schnauzer Achilles. Im grateful to him for his loyalty, love, his undying passion to protect us and heal us. "Anyone who says diamonds are a girls best friend, never had a dog."

-xo Michelle

Michelle A. Bravo

Special Thanks to:

Danielle- you helped me bring this project to life, thank you for lending me your fantastic talent.

Deborah & Alisha- thank you for your diligence and kindness- I'm so thankful for your attention to detail, your patience and your kind spirit.

The illustrator of the characters in It's me, Achilles B were done by Danielle Waterman, a very talented young artist who will be attending University of Michigan Art School in September. Her natural artistic talent and familiarity with Achilles himself has truly brought him to life in the book series. Danielle's ability to capture the heart of the character and put it on paper, is a meaningful attribute to her budding portfolio. She truly is a remarkable artist who will have boundless opportunities as she continues on her path.

It's Me, Achilles B – Moving to a new town

Mr Achilles, a large and friendly puppy will guide your child through the challenges of life such as moving, divorce, death of a pet or loved one. He has great adventures as well that are uplifting and happy and enjoys helping children with things that can be challenging for them to comprehend. Achilles is gentle, smart, happy and is chock full of great advice. Your children will fall in love with him and you will too.

Greetings! My name is Achilles B, and I just moved to town. I am friendly and I love to meet new kids so it is a pleasure to introduce myself.
The great part about moving is that I can meet nice boys and girls like you.

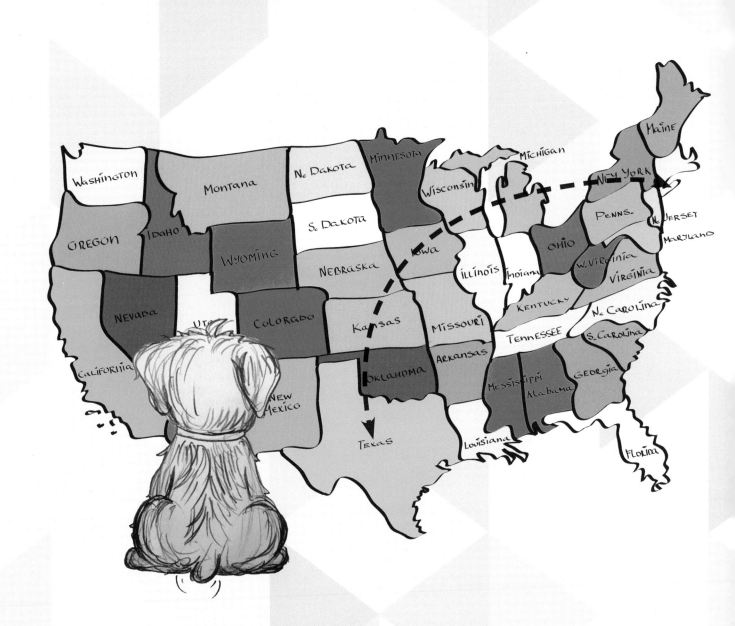

I was born in Texas. My Daddy was offered a new job so we moved to Connecticut.
I love it here, the people are kind and I now see that kids are the same no matter where I live. We love to play, laugh, dance and have silly fun. We may look different on the outside but on the inside we are all the same.

My two best friends are Christopher and Giavanna, they love to play outside, laugh with me and play sports with me.

My favorite game is hide and go seek and I am a great basketball player. It is fun learning new games and sports with my new friends. The only way to really learn about a new activity is to dive in and try it.

I love my family, My Mommy and Daddy are grownups. I have a brother and a sister. They are both older than I am. Sometimes I get mad because they are allowed to do more things than I am. Mommy says that I will grow up quickly and be able to do many more things but I get frustrated. Im just a kid, I can't help it.

It is important to treat our family members with respect and privacy. I sure learned that the hard way when I walked into my sisters room and jumped on her bed. Mommy explained to me that Giavanna has her special space, just as I have my own special space. It made sense to me once she explained it me. Having time and space to yourself is called privacy. Privacy is a nice thing to have and we all need it. My favorite private time activity is climbing on my bed, reading a book and taking a nice short nap. Oh how I love to nap.

Did I tell you we have a pet? We have a furry little cat named Coco, and she is very pretty. I love to play with her and we bought her in Massachusetts from a lady who had a house full of kittens. There were kittens up and down all over the house, it was silly. They all looked the same but we picked the happiest one.

Having a pet is a big responsibility.
It is a lot of work. My parents made us
decide what cat chore we each wanted.
I said I would play with Coco, and I have stuck to my
promise. I chase her all around the house and I like to
make her run very fast. I make sure she gets plenty
of exercise. She makes me laugh all the time.

Sometimes my parents have to go out so they hire a babysitter. I have a few different ones, but Marguerite is my favorite.

She reads to me, helps me clean up my toys, and watches movies with me. I like her very much, she is also a good friend to me. It is nice that my Mommy and Daddy have some free time to themselves.

Sometimes I go to day care. This is a place where my parents drop me off and I get a team of great babysitters in one place who are caring for other kids my age. There are fun activities, lunch time, snack time and playtime, every minute is playtime. Everyone is very friendly to me there.

I know they are always happy to see me walk through the door.

My favorite season is winter. The snow is so pretty and I love to catch snowflakes on my tongue.
My favorite thing is Snow Days.
Getting snowed in makes me hungry.
We always make pancakes on snow days.

It's time to say goodbye. I hope that you
have learned a little about me. I will see you soon.
I love sharing my childhood with you.
I can't wait to learn about you too.
We will have many fun adventures together.

-xo- Achilles B

CPSIA information can be obtained at www.ICGtesting.com
Printed in the USA
BVIW12n2325290816
460571BV00003B/3